Cars
by
Gail Saunders-Smith

Pebble Books
an imprint of Capstone Press

Pebble Books

Pebble Books are published by Capstone Press
818 North Willow Street, Mankato, Minnesota 56001
http://www.capstone-press.com
Copyright © 1998 by Capstone Press
All Rights Reserved • Printed in the United States of America

Library of Congress Cataloging-in-Publication Data
Saunders-Smith, Gail.
  Cars/by Gail Saunders-Smith.
  p.cm.
  Includes bibliographical references and index.
  Summary: In simple text and photographs, describes a
number of different cars, including toy cars, model cars,
and old cars.
  ISBN 1-56065-495-3
  1. Automobiles--Juvenile literature. [1. Automobiles.]
I. Title.

TL147.S328 1997
629.222--DC21
                          97-23581
                            CIP
                            AC

Editorial Credits
Lois Wallentine, editor; Timothy Halldin and James
Franklin, design; Michelle L. Norstad, photo research

Photo Credits
Dodge, 1, 18
Ford Motor Company, cover, 12
Unicorn Stock/Florent Flipper, 4; Dennis Thompson, 6;
  Russell R. Grundke, 8; Eric Berndt, 20
Valan Photos/Kennon Cooke, 10; V. Wilkinson, 14; John
  Mitchell, 16

9.95

Table of Contents

4

toy car

model car

play car

10

old car

new car

small car

big car

short car

long car

Words to Know

car—a type of vehicle that people use to move from one place to another

model—a toy made of plastic pieces that need to be put together

Read More

Johnstone, Michael. *Look Inside Cross-Sections: Cars.* New York: Dorling Kindersley, 1994.

Ready, Dee. *Cars.* Mankato, Minn.: Bridgestone Books, 1998.

Sutton, Richard. *Eyewitness Books: Car.* New York: Alfred A. Knopf, 1990.

Wilkenson, Sylvia. *A New True Book: Automobiles.* Chicago: Children's Press, 1982.

Internet Sites

Auto Museum—The Automotive Enthusiast Source
http://www.automuseum.com

On-Ramp Cyber Car Shows
http://www.TalkCity.com/autoonramp/carshow/carshow.html

Sloan Museum, Flint, Michigan Exhibit for WebINK
http://www.ipl.org/exhibit/sloan

Note to Parents and Teachers

This caption book illustrates and describes cars according to type, size, and shape. The noun repeats while the adjective changes on each page. The change is obvious in the photograph. The book is designed for children who are just learning how to read. Children may need assistance in using the Table of Contents, Words to Know, Read More, Internet Sites, and Index/Word List sections of the book.

Index/Word List

Word Count: 18